BARRY SANDERS:

The Elusive Icon of Detroit Football

Joseph C. Tyson

Barry Sanders

Barry Sanders

TABLE OF CONTENTS

INTRODUCTION

CHAPTER 1: EARLY YEARS

CHAPTER 2: CAREER in COLLEGE

CHAPTER 3: THE NFL DRAFT AND THE LIONS

CHAPTER 4: METHOD OF PLAYING

CHAPTER 5: SUCCESSES AND RECORDS

CHAPTER 6: RETIREMENT

CHAPTER 7: POST-FOOTBALL ACTIVITIES

CHAPTER 8: PERSONAL LIFE

CHAPTER 9: LEGACY AND IMPACT

CHAPTER 10: IMPORTANT PHRASES

CONCLUSION

INTRODUCTION

Barry Sanders is regarded as one of the best running backs in American football history, his name alone connected with explosive agility and unmatched athleticism. Sanders, who was born in Wichita, Kansas, on July 16, 1968, rose from humble origins to leave an enduring impression on the National Football League (NFL). During his illustrious career, football aficionados were attracted by his journey, which was distinguished by magnificent runs, elusive movements, and a genuine love for the game: football.

From his early years of playing football with extraordinary talent to his record-breaking accomplishments in the NFL, Sanders' narrative is one of unadulterated brilliance, tenacity, and sportsmanship. We examine the origins of his love for football, the turning points in his career, and the lasting impact he made on

Barry Sanders

and off the field as we delve into the many eras of his life.

Come along for a retrospective look at the life of Barry Sanders, a journey that goes beyond awards and stats to uncover a player whose influence is felt throughout the annals of football history.

CHAPTER 1: EARLY YEARS

Barry Sanders was born on July 16, 1968, in Wichita, Kansas, and his football career started there. Born into a close-knit family, Sanders showed an early interest in sports, especially football. He was first exposed to the game at Wichita North High School, where people soon saw his natural skill on the field.

Sanders was smaller than many of his contemporaries, but his quickness, agility, and vision made him stand out. The extraordinary accomplishments he would make in college and the workplace were predicted by his outstanding high school record. Sanders's skills on the football field were well-known, and his standout performances in high school set the stage for a career that would alter the role of running back.

Barry Sanders's early years were characterized by tenacity and an unwavering love of football, which prepared him for the remarkable career that lay ahead of him. The football world had no idea that a modest, humble young player from Wichita would soon become well-known and have a lasting impact on the game of American football.

CHAPTER 2: CAREER In COLLEGE

Barry Sanders's time in college is known for being exceptional and breaking records. Sanders played for the Cowboys from 1986 to 1988 at Oklahoma State University after having a stellar high school career.

With a performance that will never be forgotten, Sanders burst onto the college football scene in 1987 during his sophomore season. He broke several records, including the record for the most yards gained in a single season (2,628 yards), which is still in place today. Sanders was a headache for opposition teams because of his lightning-fast speed and ability to reverse direction on a dime. The Heisman Trophy, given to the best college football player in 1988, was given to him because of his electric runs and ability to turn seemingly ordinary plays into highlight reel stuff.

Barry Sanders

Sanders's choice to miss his senior year and declare for the NFL Draft signaled the end of a record-breaking college career. His tenure at Oklahoma State University is still evidence of his unparalleled talent and influence on collegiate football. Barry Sanders's professional debut raised expectations to unprecedented levels and paved the way for an unforgettable NFL career.

CHAPTER 3: THE NFL DRAFT AND THE LIONS

With his debut in the National Football League (NFL), Barry Sanders began a legendary professional career that would cement his place among the all-time best running backs. Sanders was chosen third overall by the Detroit Lions in the 1989 NFL Draft. This draft selection would turn out to be a game-changing one for the squad, as Sanders offered a special combination of quickness, dexterity, and vision to a group desperate for a game-changing playmaker.

Sanders arrived at the Lions and immediately made an impression. He won NFL Offensive Debut of the Year in 1989 after running for 1,470 yards and 14 touchdowns in his debut season, showcasing his tremendous talent. The Lions' offense soon came to be known for Sanders'

Barry Sanders

elusive flips and darting jukes that left opponents in his wake.

From 1989 to 1998, the whole time he was a member of the Detroit Lions, Sanders put up outstanding performances. He rose to prominence as the team's face, winning multiple awards and being selected for ten Pro Bowls and six First-Team All-Pro selections. Sanders finished as the NFL's second-all-time leading rusher at the time of his retirement despite facing defenses that were designed to stop him.

Sanders never achieved championship-caliber team success, but his influence on the Detroit Lions and the league at large much outweighed his achievements. Being one of the most captivating and adored athletes to ever play on the gridiron, he established an enduring legacy during his time in Detroit and cemented his place in football history.

CHAPTER 4: METHOD OF PLAYING

Gaming Approach:

Barry Sanders' style of play combines vision, agility, and a remarkable ability to outmaneuver opponents. Despite being underappreciated because of his height (5 feet 8 inches), Sanders had a huge influence on the field. His trademark maneuvers—quick spins, unexpected jives, and evasive cuts—became legendary, leaving rivals gasping for air.

Sanders was unique not only for his lightning-fast speed but also for his unmatched ability to shift directions with almost otherworldly agility. His athleticism could turn an ordinary running play into a highlight-reel moment that would astound fans and defenders alike. Sanders was able to maneuver through confined places with ease thanks to his low center of gravity and balance, which created opportunities where none seemed to exist.

Barry Sanders

In addition to his physical prowess, Sanders had a keen football sense. His ability to see defenders' movements on the field allowed him to make snap decisions that frequently left his opponents lagging. In addition to redefining the running back position, his playmaking style produced a highlight reel that still fascinates football fans today.

Barry Sanders was a running back who inspired many future running backs and left an enduring impression on the game with his unique blend of athleticism and elegance. His ability to make the remarkable seem ordinary is still evidence of his special and lasting influence in the football community.

CHAPTER 5: SUCCESSES AND RECORDS

Throughout his brilliant career, Barry Sanders set numerous records and accomplished a great deal, demonstrating his supremacy on the football field. Among the noteworthy highlights are:

1. Heisman Trophy (1988): After an incredible season at Oklahoma State University, Sanders was named the winner of the coveted Heisman Trophy, which is given to the finest college football player.

2. NFL Offensive Rookie of the Year (1989): After racking up 1,470 running yards and 14 touchdowns in his first season with the Detroit Lions, Sanders was named the NFL Offensive Rookie of the Year.

3. Ten Pro Bowl Selections: Sanders' ten NFL seasons saw him selected for the Pro Bowl, which is evidence of his consistent success throughout his career.

Barry Sanders

4. Six First-Team All-Pro Selections: Throughout his career, Sanders was selected six times for the First-Team All-Pro, a testament to his steady standing as one of the league's best running backs.

5. Four NFL Rushing Titles: Sanders' extraordinary ability to continually outperform his contemporaries was demonstrated by his four NFL Rushing Titles (1990, 1994, 1996, 1997).

6. 2,053-Yard Rushing Season (1997): With 2,053 rushing yards at the end of the 1997 season, Sanders accomplished the uncommon distinction of rushing for more than 2,000 yards in a single season.

7. 15,269 Career Rushing Yards: Barry Sanders' endurance and unwavering performance were demonstrated at the time of his retirement when he was the second-best rusher in NFL history.

Barry Sanders

Although these accomplishments offer some insight into Sanders' extraordinary career, they don't fully capture the influence he had on football as a sport. His accomplishments and records cemented his reputation as one of the best running backs to ever play in the NFL.

CHAPTER 6: RETIREMENT

On July 27, 1999, Barry Sanders unexpectedly announced his retirement from the NFL, shocking the football community. Sanders had just turned 31 years old and had just finished a season in which he had gained more than 15,000 rushing yards in his career. Fans and fellow players alike reacted to his decision to retire from the game with a range of emotions and conjecture.

Sanders decided to announce his retirement by faxing a statement to his local newspaper, the Wichita Eagle, which made it a very unusual move. He said in the statement that he wanted to exit the game on his terms and that the Detroit Lions' losing culture had an impact on his choice. After ten years of amazing performances, his departure signaled the end of an era for the Lions and left a vacuum in the hearts of the fans.

Barry Sanders

Though many felt that Sanders retired too soon, his legacy lived on. As the third all-time leading rusher when he left the NFL, his impact on the game was immortalized, and his exit became a significant event in football history. Sanders left a vacancy in the Detroit backfield that was evidence of both his unique talent and the impact he had on the team and the league at large.

CHAPTER 7: POST-FOOTBALL ACTIVITIES

Following his retirement from the NFL, Barry Sanders made a smooth transition into a variety of non-football endeavors, demonstrating his adaptability and ongoing influence offline. Among the noteworthy facets of his life after football are:

1. Sanders ventured into the world of business and engaged in several endeavors. This included collaborations with businesses and projects that benefited from his reputation and football knowledge.

2. Sanders ventured into the realm of sports broadcasting, offering his insights and evaluations for football-oriented shows. The stories around the game gained substance from his observations and direct experience.

3. Philanthropy: Using his position to support charity causes, Sanders actively participated in philanthropic endeavors. He supported community development efforts and youth education programs, among other things.

4. Authorship: In his autobiography, "Barry Sanders: Now You See Him...," Sanders provides readers with an insight into his personal and professional life, as well as the choices that molded his incredible football career.

5. Public Appearances: Sanders continued to be in high demand for appearances in public, taking part in talks, conferences, and interviews that gave him the chance to impart his knowledge and perspectives to a wider audience.

After leaving football, Barry Sanders remained a well-respected person in the sports and business industries. His multifaceted outlook on life beyond football showed a dedication to having a good influence and contributing to a variety of domains outside of the football field.

CHAPTER 8: PERSONAL LIFE

In general, Barry Sanders has avoided the harsh glare that frequently comes with being a football star by leading a private existence. He has a reputation for being reserved and has kept many aspects of his private life hidden from the public.

As a devoted family man, Sanders has raised four children with his wife, Lauren Campbell. His career and post-football life have demonstrated his unwavering devotion to family values.

Sanders has maintained a degree of privacy in his personal life that is unusual for a person of his caliber, even in the face of the notoriety and accolades he received during his football career. This deliberate decision to maintain a low profile off the field has added to the renowned running back's aura of mystery.

Barry Sanders

Beyond the numbers and accomplishments, there is a person who values a quiet existence away from the spotlight, and while fans and the media respect Sanders' need for seclusion, it also serves as a reminder.

CHAPTER 9: LEGACY AND IMPACT

In the realm of football, Barry Sanders' legacy goes beyond numbers and records; it is evidence of his unwavering character, dynamic play style, and enduring influence on the game. Here are some salient features of his lasting legacy:

1. Redefining the Running Back Position: With his unmatched agility, quick change of direction, and elusive running style, Sanders completely changed the running back position. His impact on the next generation of running backs is demonstrated by their attempts to imitate his on-field maneuvers.

2. Unmatched Records and Achievements: From his 2,053-yard rushing season to his eleven Pro Bowl appearances and other honors, Sanders' name is inscribed in the NFL record books. His accomplishments and

records continue to set the standard for greatness in the league.

3. Football legend for the Detroit Lions: Sanders' time with the team cemented his standing as a team icon. He stuck with the squad through thick and thin, becoming the team's face and winning over supporters who continue to honor his accomplishments.

4. Impact on Culture: Sanders made a lasting impression on popular culture outside of the field. With his highlight-reel runs and unique flair, he became a cultural phenomenon that captivated spectators and went beyond the boundaries of sports.

5. Model of Sportsmanship: Sanders demonstrated professionalism and sportsmanship both on and off the field. Fans, rivals, and teammates all admired him for his work ethic, modesty, and respect for the game.

6. Impact on Upcoming Generations: Sanders' influence is felt in the guidance and motivation he offers to

Barry Sanders

budding sportsmen. The running backs, who credit him with inspiring and influencing them in their careers, carry on his legacy.

American football is a sport that we view and enjoy differently because of Barry Sanders' legacy, which extends beyond the football field and is a story of excellence, humility, and tenacity.

CHAPTER 10: IMPORTANT PHRASES

Barry Sanders, despite his tendency toward reserve, has offered observations and insights that sum up his philosophy of life and the game. Here are some well-known statements ascribed to him:

1. "I just try to do the best job I can and make the best decisions I can."

2. "Football is like life. It calls for tenacity, self-control, diligence, sacrifice, commitment, and deference to authority."

3. "When you have great coaches, then after you have great coaches you get great players. You tell them one thing and you have an excellent organization.'"

4. "You know, I've never said to myself, 'Hey, I want to be here in five years.'" I've consistently declared, "Hey,

Barry Sanders

I'm going to stick to who I am, and hopefully that will take care of the future.'"

5. "I was very fortunate to play for the Lions and be a part of that organization."

These quotations shed light on Barry Sanders' philosophy by highlighting ideas of tenacity, commitment, and remaining loyal to oneself. The values that led him both on and off the football field are reflected in them.

CONCLUSION

Barry Sanders is regarded as a gridiron legend who has had a lasting impact on football. From the Wichita fields to the NFL's highest position, his career is a tale of unmatched athleticism, humility, and a playing style that transformed the running back position. Beyond records and stats, Sanders' legacy includes cultural significance, serving as a role model for sportsmanship, and having a lasting impact on upcoming athletic generations.

Sanders distinguished himself with a unique blend of speed, agility, and vision throughout his career, which included winning the Heisman Trophy as a collegiate player and setting records in the NFL with the Detroit Lions. His choice to leave the game on his terms by retiring in his prime emphasizes his devotion to maintaining the aura surrounding his career.

Barry Sanders

Away from the field, Sanders's quiet but significant personal life demonstrates a devotion to philanthropy and family. His post-football pursuits in philanthropy, business, and television show that he has a flexible and well-rounded outlook on life outside of football.

Barry Sanders' legacy extends beyond the awards and recognition he received; it is preserved in his highlight-reel moments, his long-lasting influence on the Detroit Lions, and the motivation he now offers to young sportsmen. His tale serves as a tribute to the tenacity, desire, and capacity to push the boundaries of what is thought to be achievable in sports. Barry Sanders is still revered as an icon, a testament to excellence woven into the rich tapestry of American football history, as both players and onlookers may still vividly recall his evasive runs.

Made in the USA
Monee, IL
19 December 2023

49809789R00017